Dirt Bikes

By John Hamilton

VISIT US AT
WWW.ABDOPUBLISHING.COM

Published by ABDO Publishing Company, PO Box 398166, Minneapolis, MN 55439.
Copyright ©2014 by Abdo Consulting Group, Inc. International copyrights reserved
in all countries. No part of this book may be reproduced in any form without written
permission from the publisher. A&D Xtreme™ is a trademark and logo of
ABDO Publishing Company.

Printed in the United States of America, North Mankato, Minnesota.
102013
012014

 PRINTED ON RECYCLED PAPER

Editor: Sue Hamilton
Graphic Design: Sue Hamilton
Cover Design: John Hamilton
Cover Photo: Corbis
Interior Photos: American Honda Motor Company-pgs 8-9, 10-11 & 28-29;
AP-pgs 20-21; Corbis-pgs 32; Dreamstime-pgs 6-7 & 14-15; Getty-pgs 18-19 & 22-23;
iStock-pgs 12-13; Kurt Glenn-pgs 4-5, 16-17, 24-25 & 26-27;
Thinkstock-pgs 1, 2-3 & 30-31.

ABDO Booklinks
Web sites about motorcycles are featured on our Book Links
pages. These links are routinely monitored and updated to
provide the most current information available.
Web site: www.abdopublishing.com

Library of Congress Control Number: 2013946166

Cataloging-in-Publication Data

Hamilton, John, 1959-
 Dirt bikes / John Hamilton.
    p. cm. -- (Xtreme motorcycles)
Includes index.
ISBN 978-1-62403-219-6
1. Trail bikes--Juvenile literature.   I. Title.
629.227/5--dc23

2013946166

Contents

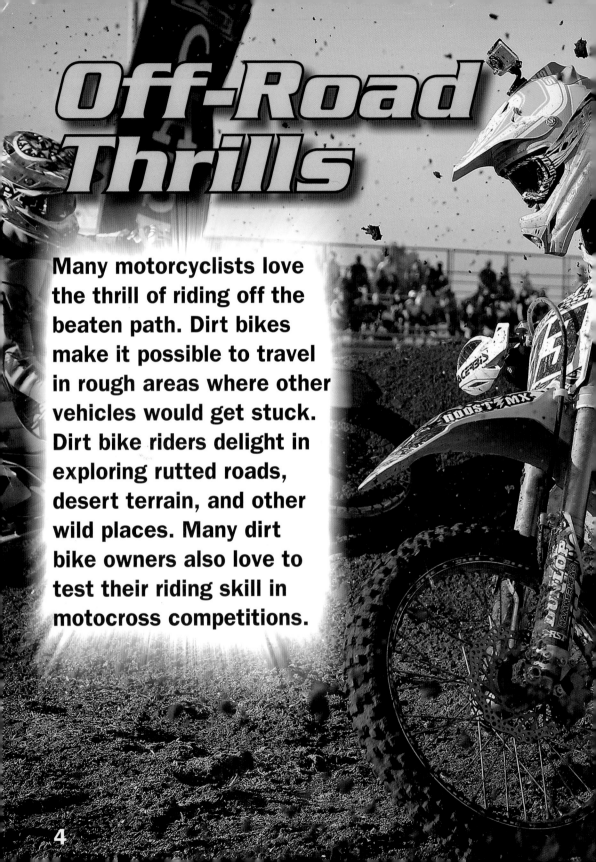

Off-Road Thrills

Many motorcyclists love the thrill of riding off the beaten path. Dirt bikes make it possible to travel in rough areas where other vehicles would get stuck. Dirt bike riders delight in exploring rutted roads, desert terrain, and other wild places. Many dirt bike owners also love to test their riding skill in motocross competitions.

What is a Dirt Bike?

Dirt bikes are motorcycles built for traveling off-road, on dirt paths, or on rough terrain. They are simple and light vehicles compared with road machines such as cruisers or sport bikes. Dirt bikes are built with rugged frames, knobby tires, and high ground clearance for traveling on the roughest roads.

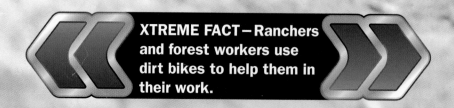

XTREME FACT—Ranchers and forest workers use dirt bikes to help them in their work.

Parts of a Dirt Bike

Subframe

Seat

Muffler Exhaust System

Rear Brake

HONDA

Swingarm

2014 HONDA CRF450R

Handlebars

Steering Damper

Fender

Front Fork

Front Suspension

Front Brake

449cc
Engine

Knobby Tire

Engine

The size of dirt bike engines ranges from about 60 cc to 600 cc. The larger displacement engines give plenty of power for such lightweight bikes.
Dirt bike engines are placed high on the frame. This gives the engines lots of room, or clearance, so they don't strike obstacles on uneven terrain.

Dirt bike engines are either two-stroke or four-stroke. Two-stroke engines have more power and are easier to fix. Four-stroke engines are more fuel efficient and pollute less. Because of environmental concerns, the recent trend in dirt bike design has been four-stroke engines.

XTREME FACT — Because of all the dust and dirt kicked up by off-road bikes, their engines are equipped with large air filters. The air filters keep debris from getting sucked into the engines and clogging them.

Chassis

The chassis, or frame, of a dirt bike is usually made of aluminum. This metal is much more lightweight than steel, which is used on cruiser motorcycles. Most dirt bikes weigh less than 300 pounds (136 kg). Because they are so lightweight, dirt bikes can go fast, even though they are powered by smaller engines than most cruisers or other street bikes.

Tires

Dirt bikes are equipped with tires that have lots of bumps for gripping loose dirt or muddy roads and paths. This increased traction is especially important during racing competition.

These kind of tires are called "nobbies." The raised rubber knobs dig into the ground, helped by the weight of the bike. This gives maximum traction on loose surfaces, but not very good grip on paved roads.

Motocross

Many dirt bike owners love to race against fellow riders. Motocross is a kind of race that is held on an outdoor off-road track.

XTREME FACT – Supercross is a more challenging version of motocross. Tracks are usually built in large stadiums.

Motocross tracks are short. They range in length from .5 to 2 miles (.8 to 3.2 km). They include challenging obstacles such as jumps, rollers, and tables.

Motocross competition is divided into classes. The size of a dirt bike's engine determines in which class it will race. In many major competitions, there is also a class reserved for women racers.

Freestyle

Freestyle motocross is also known as FMX. During competition, riders try to get high scores by performing daredevil midair stunts. These death-defying tricks have colorful names such as Cliffhanger, Lazy Boy, and Hart Attack. Judges score each rider based on difficulty and style.

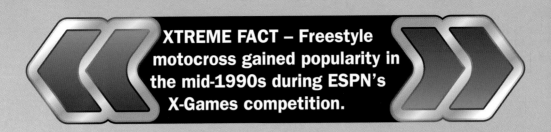

XTREME FACT – Freestyle motocross gained popularity in the mid-1990s during ESPN's X-Games competition.

Cliffhanger

Heel Clicker

Lazy Boy

One-Handed Hart Attack

Safety Gear

Motocross racing and off-road riding can be very dangerous. Dirt bike riders wear special safety gear. Colorful, lightweight helmets are made of Kevlar, fiberglass, and carbon fiber. These "lids" protect a rider's head and face.

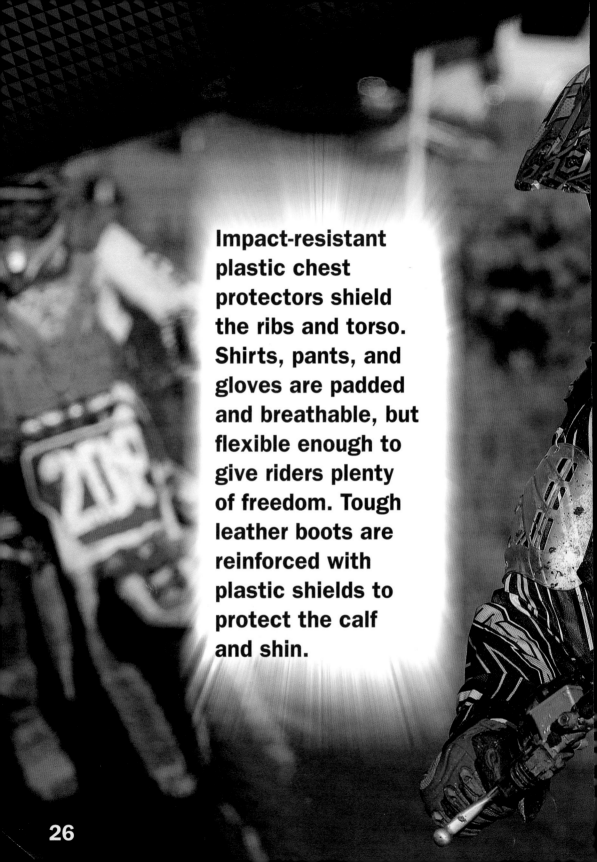

Impact-resistant plastic chest protectors shield the ribs and torso. Shirts, pants, and gloves are padded and breathable, but flexible enough to give riders plenty of freedom. Tough leather boots are reinforced with plastic shields to protect the calf and shin.

Dual-Sport

Dual-sport motorcycles are designed for off-road riding, and are also legal to ride on paved roads. These "street-legal" bikes are based on dirt bike designs but also include equipment such as mirrors, lights, and instruments. These add-ons allow them to be ridden in normal traffic.

2013 Honda CRF250L

XTREME FACT – Dual-sport bikes are also called "on-off" bikes or "dualies."

Glossary

CC (Cubic Centimeters)

Engines are often compared by measuring the amount of space (displacement) inside the cylinders where gas and air mix and are ignited to produce power. Displacement is measured in cubic centimeters.

Cruiser

A type of motorcycle where the rider sits in a laid-back posture with arms and feet forward. The Harley-Davidson company is known for its cruiser motorcycles.

ESPN

A television channel that broadcasts entertainment and sports programming.

Kevlar

A light and very strong man-made fiber. It is used to make helmets, vests, and other protective gear for sports, military, and law enforcement personnel.

Roller

On a motocross track, 1- to 2-foot (30-61 cm) -tall dirt mounds placed very close together.

Rollers →

Sport Bikes

A type of motorcycle that is built for quick acceleration, fast speeds, and superior cornering on paved roads. These types of motorcycles are typically less comfortable for the rider.

Table

In motocross, a jump with a flat top.

Terrain

The physical features of a section of land.

Traction

The grip of a vehicle's tires on the road or ground.

X-Games

Extreme sporting events, such as motocross competitions, that are broadcast each year in the summer and winter by the ESPN television network.

Index